WESTMINSTER PUBLIC LIBRARY
3020 01118 0535

D0793768

CULTURES CONNECT US!

FESTIVALS AND CELEBRATIONS

BY CYRIL BASSINGTON

Gareth Stevens PUBLISHING

Please visit our website, www.garethstevens.com. For a free color catalog of all our high-quality books, call toll free 1-800-542-2595 or fax 1-877-542-2596.

Cataloging-in-Publication Data

Names: Bassington, Cyril.
Title: Festivals and celebrations / Cyril Bassington.
Description: New York : Gareth Stevens Publishing, 2020. | Series: Cultures connect us! | Includes glossary and index.
Identifiers: ISBN 9781538238349 (pbk.) | ISBN 9781538238363 (library bound) | ISBN 9781538238356 (6 pack)
Subjects: LCSH: Festivals–Juvenile literature. | Holidays–Juvenile literature.
Classification: LCC GT3933.B374 2020 | DDC 394.26–dc23

Published in 2020 by
Gareth Stevens Publishing
111 East 14th Street, Suite 349
New York, NY 10003

Designer: Reann Nye
Editor: Therese Shea

Photo credits: series art (background) Lukasz Szwaj/Shutterstock.com; cover toonman/Shutterstock.com; p. 5 Rawpixel.com/Shutterstock.com; p. 7 skynesher/E+/Getty Images; p. 9 Golden Pixels LLC/Shutterstock.com; p. 11 Aliii/Shutterstock.com; p. 13 Christian Kober/robertharding/Getty Images; p. 15 Bastiaan Slabbers/iStock Unreleased/Getty Images; p. 17 Jasmin Merdan/Moment/Getty Images; p. 19 Monkey Business Images/Shutterstock.com; p. 21 yongtick/Shutterstock.com.

Printed in the United States of America

CPSIA compliance information: Batch #CS19GS: For further information contact Gareth Stevens, New York, New York at 1-800-542-2595.

CONTENTS

Boldface words appear in the glossary.

So Much to Celebrate!

Do you live in a community of many cultures? A culture is a group of people with certain beliefs and ways of life. This includes foods, clothes, music, **religion**, and much more! You can learn a lot about cultures from their **celebrations**.

Giving Thanks

Celebrations and **festivals** tell us what matters to cultures. For example, Thanksgiving is a time set aside to be thankful for family, friends, and food. It's celebrated by Americans and Canadians. Other countries set aside days for giving thanks, too.

Looking Back at History

Some celebrations are just 1 day, like Thanksgiving is. Some are many days. Hanukkah is celebrated over 8 nights, often in December. People light candles on a **menorah** to remember a special event in Jewish history. Hanukkah is also called the Festival of Lights.

Honoring Independence

Some celebrations have to do with honoring a country's history. Independence Day, also called the Fourth of July, honors when the United States became an independent, or free, country. Canada Day, which is July 1, celebrates when Canada became independent.

Remembering Their Dead

Many cultures remember loved ones who have died on special days. Día de los Muertos (DEE-ah DEH LOHS MUEHR-tohs), or Day of the Dead, is a holiday that began in Mexico. People **decorate** the graves of their loved ones.

Celebrating Freedom

Today, Juneteenth is celebrated all over the United States, but it first began in Texas. On June 19, people remember when slaves in that state learned they were free and that slavery had been **abolished**. Celebrations include prayers, parades, music, dancing, and food.

From Fasting to Feasting

The **Muslim** festival of Eid al-Fitr (EED uhl-FIHT-uhr) marks the end of the holy month of **fasting** called Ramadan. Praying, sharing special meals, gift giving, and visiting the graves of loved ones are part of the holiday.

Changing Celebrations

Cultures are always changing, especially in a community of many cultures. Festivals and celebrations change, too. Halloween was once about chasing away bad spirits—not collecting candy! However, holidays are a great way to remember a culture's past and celebrate its future.

Shared Values

Cultures often value the same things, like family. They also often have **traditions** in common, like parades. Have you ever celebrated Chinese New Year? It's a time for family and parades! Take part in a celebration like this and learn about another culture!

GLOSSARY

abolish: to officially end something

celebration: a time to show happiness for an event through activities such as eating or playing music

decorate: to make something look nice by adding extra items to it

fast: to eat no food for a period of time

festival: a special time or event when people gather to celebrate something

menorah: an object that holds seven or nine candles and that is used in Jewish worship

Muslim: having to do with the religion of Islam

religion: a belief in and way of honoring a god or gods

tradition: a long-practiced custom or way of behaving

FOR MORE INFORMATION

BOOKS

Carpentiere, Elizabeth Crooker. *Festivals Around the World.* Peterborough, NH: Cobblestone Publishing Company, 2017.

Lawrence, Sandra. *Festivals and Celebrations.* Wilton, CT: 360 Degrees, 2017.

Rissman, Rebecca. *Festivals.* Chicago, IL: Capstone Raintree, 2014.

WEBSITES

Multicultural Dates—World Culture Celebrations

www.globalkidsoz.com.au/multicultural_dates.php

See which culture is celebrating something today!

Winter Celebrations

kids.nationalgeographic.com/explore/winter-celebrations/

Learn more about winter holidays including Kwanzaa and Chinese New Year.

INDEX